Encounters with the Other

How we continue to misunderstand, dehumanize,
scorn, humiliate, oppress,
and even kill other humans.

And how we can stop.

Barry Oshry

Published in this edition in 2024 by:
Triarchy Press
Axminster, England

info@triarchypress.net
www.triarchypress.net

ISBN: 978-1-911193-48-7

To the Peacemakers

Until we see the Other with new eyes and curb our addiction to
belief in our own superiority, fear not:
your work will be in demand.

Foreword

1.

I was a child
when I first learned of the Horror.
It frightened me.
Mother, I cried,
Could it be true?
Go out and play, she said,
and that was all she said.
Father, I tried,
Could it be true?
Do your homework, he said,
and that was all he said.
Grandpa, I asked,
Could it be true?
He looked into my eyes and said...slowly:
Do you really want to know?
And then he spoke.
And I was no longer afraid.
Now I was angry.
How, grandpa,
How could people be so evil, so cruel, so ignorant
to do such terrible things to others?

2.

Then I grew up,
played different games,
thought different thoughts,
yet the one thought remained:
How could people do this?

3.

As I grew older,
I learned of other horrors,
many other horrors,
from our earliest history
to today's news,
from countries north, east, south, and west.
Hundreds of millions dead
always for allegedly "good" reasons.
In time my question changed –
not the words,
just the tone.
Can you hear it the new way I heard it?
Not in anger
but as puzzlement,
as a mystery to be unraveled.
Try, if you can, to hear it that way:
as inquiry
How could people do this?
How does it begin?
When and from whom do they learn it?
Questions I pondered,
for many years I pondered,
until, in time,
I sat down and wrote
Encounters with the Other.

Act I

How our Culture and the Culture
of the "Other" came to be

1.

Many cultures may look strange to us,
but not to the "others".
And our culture may look strange to the "others"
but not to us.
That simple fact is the beginning of understanding.

2.

We may feel that our culture is simply
the way things have been, are, and ought to be.
The "others" likely feel the same way
about their culture.

3.

We and the "others" were not born
with the rules of our cultures;
we learned them
from parents and elders,
teachers, and peers,
and media.

4.

In both cultures
we and the "others" absorbed
the do's and don'ts of our cultures –
appropriate and inappropriate emotionality,
ways of speaking,
clothing,
interacting with elders and
people of different sexes,
and much more.
We were taught our culture's beliefs and values,
rites and rituals,
ways of solving problems,
seeking justice,
expressing joy, or sadness, or grief,
and much more.

5.

In both cultures, these rules were taught
as the ways to live, to survive,
the ways to be in the world.

6.

In time, we and the "others" learn our rules so well
that we no longer experience them as rules,
they become the lenses through which we view the world.
Except we don't see our lens
and how it shapes what we see.
Instead, we believe we see the world
as it *really* is.

7.
Neither we nor the "others"
experience our culture as an option,
as one of many possibilities.
Each of us experiences our culture as
the way things are or ought to be.
And then we meet.

Act II
Our Culture Encounters the "Other"

Loose and Tight, Liberal and Conservative, Pure and Conflicted, Tolerance and Purity Solutions

1.

So now our culture encounters the "other".
The "other" may have immigrated to our culture.
Or we may have conquered them.
Or they may have once been invisible in our culture,
and now they have become prominent.

2.

Through our cultural lens
the cultural behavior of the "other" appears
    strange
    off
    wrong
    inappropriate.
Wrong language, dress, emotionality, skin color, rites and
rituals, and so on.

3.

Since our cultural rules are experienced
as the way to live, to survive, to be,
the cultural behavior of the "other" is experienced
as upsetting of our culture,
as weakening it,
or coarsening it,
and, potentially, as threatening its survival.
And we react.

4.

Loose and **Tight**

Sometimes we react reflexively
to the cultural behavior of the "other".
At times we go **Loose**.
We reflexively allow the behavior of the "others",
not because we love the "others" or respect them or value their behavior,
but because our reflexive Looseness allows us to avoid the discomfort of dealing with the complexity raised by their presence.

At times we go **Tight**.
We reflexively reject the behavior of the "other",
we judge it negatively, dismiss it, afford it no legitimate place in our culture.
Our reflexive dismissal again allows us to avoid the discomfort of dealing with the complexity raised by the "other's" presence.

5.

Loose and **Tight** appear in conflict with one another,
yet both arise out of the same condition:
discomfort in responding to the encounter with the "other".

6.

Liberal and **Conservative**

Loose and Tight are *knee-jerk* responses to the "other";
Liberal and Conservative are *values-based* responses.
The **Liberal** response is based on moral grounds.
It is offered as the right thing to do,
to bring in the poor, the displaced, the oppressed.
Liberals believe that the current culture
will be strengthened, spiritually if not economically,
by including the "others";
and they believe that the "others" will be strengthened
by their inclusion.

The **Conservative** response is also based on moral grounds –
the primacy of preserving and protecting the existing culture.
Conservatives value the culture as it is,
and believe that including the "others"
will weaken, distort, pollute, and potentially destroy the culture,
while diminishing the value of their own position within the culture.

Liberals and **Conservatives** oppose one another.
The opposition is often intense
since each stands on firm moral grounds.

7.
The **Pure**.

Some of us are **pure** Liberal,
firm in our conviction that making room for the "other"
is clearly the right thing to do;
while others of us are **pure** Conservative,
equally firm in our conviction that preserving our culture
is the right thing to do.

8.
The **Conflicted**.

Many of us experience ourselves as Liberal or Conservative… mostly,
yet at times find ourselves **conflicted**.
We experience ourselves primarily as Conservative,
yet at times, find ourselves welcoming and feeling generous
toward the "other".
Others of us experience ourselves primarily as Liberal,
yet at times find ourselves judging and rejecting the behavior of
the "other".

9.
Tolerance and **Purity** Solutions

Sometimes,
out of Looseness or Liberalism,
the "other" is *allowed* to co-exist in the host culture,
in a *tolerable* state of tension,
with various restrictions and limitations,
amid forces for accepting the "other"
and forces for rejecting them,
between living peaceably with them
or oppressing them,
between occasional acts of violence

and subsequent reconciliations.
Such tolerable states of tension can last
for years, decades, and even centuries.
This is a culture's **tolerance** solution to the encounter with the "other".

Sometimes,
out of Tightness or Conservatism,
the forces to reject the "other"
overwhelm the forces to accept them.
The "other" is experienced as too different, foreign, dangerous.
The potential or continued existence of the "other" in the host culture
is seen as weakening, polluting, distorting, and threatening to destroy it.
The solution is to protect and preserve the culture by
confining, suppressing, exiling, or destroying the "other".
This is a culture's **purity** solution to the encounter with the "other".

10.
And, at times,
Tolerance solutions
are overwhelmed by **Purity** solutions,
resulting in catastrophe for the "other".

11.
Dehumanizing the Oppressed and the Oppressor

Both the Purity and Tolerance Solutions
diminish the **oppressed**,
(at times, disastrously);
yet they also diminish the **oppressors**,
corrupting and de-humanizing them
as they hang their self-worth on the fragile thread
of the diminished worth of the "other".

What else is possible?

Assimilation

1.

Sometimes the "other" finds acceptance
by adapting to and adopting the cultural rules of the host culture.
And sometimes the "others" achieve full assimilation
when they become indistinguishable from the host.

2.

Some "others" can never become indistinguishable, or their
progress to indistinguishability can be slowed because of skin
color, dress, religion, racial characteristics or sexual identity;
and still "others" have no interest in becoming
indistinguishable.

3.

And sometimes what feels like assimilation
is simply a Tolerance solution;
and, given the right mix of circumstances –
diminished resources, threat of warfare,
all enflamed by demagoguery –
assimilation/Tolerance readily devolves into a Purity solution.

4.

And the final limitation of assimilation
is the grand assumption
that the host culture is the best of all cultures –
and that, therefore, assimilation is the obvious solution.
Why wouldn't everyone want to be just like us?

Knowing/not Knowing the "Other"

1.

Substitute knowledge

We sincerely believe we know the "other",
and that knowledge justifies our feelings and actions toward them.
But consider for a moment the possibility that we *do not* know them –
not really,
not the "others" generally (if there is such)
and certainly not *this* "other"
who stands before us.
And consider the possibility that,
in the absence of real knowledge,
our minds are open to
"substitute knowledge"
– our projections based on our own fears and desires –
(seeing *them* as thieves, liars, cheats, sexual menaces).

And consider the possibility that in the absence of real
knowing,
our minds are open to "substitute knowledge"
as fed to us by demagogues –
enflaming us with images of the "other" –
their conspiracies, vile practices, inferiority,
all in contrast to our purity.
"Substitute knowledge" fills the void.
With it we now *know* the "other",
and knowing what we know:
Who wouldn't do what we do to such people?

Nothing else is possible

1.

So, maybe nothing else is possible.
Maybe we are at the mercy of our genetically transmitted
wariness of the "other",
triggering us into fight or flight.
Loose and Tight
Liberal and Conservative
Tolerance and Purity
snap reactions,
snap judgments,
drawing us ever more closely into like-minded tribes,
reinforcing one another with our funds of substitute knowledge,
growing ever more different and separate from the "other".
Circumstances will arrive,
as they are arriving now.
Wars, revolutions, environmental disasters.
Millions on the move,
different colors, religions, languages, politics;
the demagogues are at their microphones and twitter feeds,
the message is clear;
it's an old one;
it's been here throughout the ages.
Save our tribe!
Purity, purity, purity!
What else is possible?
What about laws?
Can laws stop oppression?

Laws

1.

The Law

One way to end oppression
is to pass laws forbidding it,
or issue proclamations and emancipations
indicating that the "other"
is free and equal and welcome.

2.

Laws and proclamations can serve the "other"
when, in the midst of acts of oppression,
they can point to and draw on the laws and proclamations
for relief or justice.

3.

Yet laws and proclamations often fail
to stop oppressors
who continue to see the "other"
as foreign, as a danger, as a pollutant
who needs to be controlled,
suppressed, exiled, or eliminated,
despite the law.

4.

Laws, proclamations, and emancipations
cannot change how we *see* the "other";
they may control our behavior,
but they do not control our *seeing*.
Can anything change how we see the other?
Is it possible to really *see* the "other?"

Act III:
Seeing the "Other"

Through Power or Love

1.

What do we see when we see the "other"?
Do we see them as like us
or as different from us,
as connected to us
or as separate from us?

2.

Power seeing
is seeing difference
and separateness.
*The "others" are different from us
and unconnected to us.*

Love seeing
is seeing commonality
and connectedness.
*The "others" are like us
and connected to us.*

3.
Robustly seeing the "other"

It is possible, theoretically at least, for our experience of the "other"
to be grounded in *both* Power *and* Love;
where we experience our differences from the "other"
and our commonality with them,
our separateness from them
and our connectedness with them.
Robust seeing is a possibility,
yet it is a possibility too rarely realized,
and here may be why.

4.
The Power reflex

Is it not true
that, when we encounter cultural behavior of the "other"
that is very different from our own –
dress, religion, language, emotionality, rites and rituals –
our *reflex response* – without awareness or choice –
is to experience our difference from the "others"
more than our commonality with them?
Our separateness from them
more than our connectedness with them?
This is not a question of what is right or wrong,
moral or immoral,
Liberal or Conservative.
It is a question about our *reflex response*
to the different cultural behavior of the "other".

5.
Power without Love

The reflex preference for Power,
when it happens,
can easily set off a process in which
Power gradually increases its predominance over Love,
eventually overcoming it
to the point at which Love is gone,
and there is no experience of commonality or connectedness
with the "other".
And here is how that happens.

6.
A vicious cycle: Separate and different

Separateness and difference
are the two components of Power,
with each reinforcing the other.
The more we maintain our separateness from the "other",
the more this supports our experience of difference from them.
And experiencing our difference from them
reinforces our inclination to remain separate from them.
And round and round we go,
separateness enhancing difference
which reinforces separateness,
and downward to the experience of
Power without Love.

7.

Power without Love

When our experience is grounded in
Power without Love,
we lose all commonality and connectedness
with the "other",
enabling us to do things to the "other"
we would never do to one another –
suppress them, enslave them, exile them,
and murder them.

8.

Love to the rescue?

So, where is Love?
When our experience of the "other" is grounded in Love,
we experience our commonality with the "other"
and our connectedness with them.
If our experience of the "other" were grounded in Love,
the likelihood of bigotry, oppression, and rejection
would be greatly diminished,
if not eliminated.
It's not so easy to oppress people
with whom we feel so much in common
and with whom we are jointly engaged.
So where is Love?

9.
You can't get there from here... not easily

Once we are locked into the experience of Power without Love,
Love is not experienced as a possibility.
Good idea maybe, but not with these people!
Once we fall into Power without Love,
our experience of the "other" as irreconcilably foreign
feels solid, a reflection of reality.
This is who they *really* are.
All efforts to change are seen as foolish, pointless, dangerous.
Not with these people.
All of this happens without awareness or thought.
All of this is a consequence of our system blindness.

10.
System blindness, system sight

In our human interactions
we are constantly falling in and out of
patterns of relationship with others;
Power without Love is one such pattern.
Here is what we need to know:
The patterns we fall into shape how we experience ourselves and others.

When we are blind to systems,
we believe that our experience of the "other"
is a reflection of reality –
This is who they really are.

When we have system sight,
we understand that how we experience the "other"
is a *consequence* of the pattern we have fallen into.
Change the pattern and our experience of them will likely change.

When we are blind to systems,
we think that the realistic way to deal with our relationship
with the "other"
is to dominate, oppress, suppress, exile, or destroy them.
Who wouldn't do this to such people?

When we have system sight,
we think that the realistic way to deal with our relationship
with the "other"
is to change the pattern of relationship we have fallen into.
In this case, this means infusing Love into "Power without
Love".

11.
Love as the disrupter

We have seen the self-reinforcing pattern of
Power without Love –
how being separate from the "other"
reinforces our experience of their being different from us;
and experiencing them as being different from us
reinforces our staying apart,
and round and round it goes.
Love needs to be the disrupter of this cycle.
Separateness needs to be counterbalanced with connectedness.
We need to connect with the "other"
in *ongoing and mutually meaningful ways* –
building housing together,
taking meals together,
plowing fields together,
writing and producing plays together,
working on community projects together.
Endless possibilities of connecting in *ongoing and mutually
meaningful ways.*

12.
The Love cycle: Part 1

For Love also has its cycle.
The two components of Love are
connectedness – partnering together in common enterprise –
and *commonality* – experiencing our fundamental similarity
with the "other".
Each component reinforces the other –
partnering – working together with the "other" –
increases the likelihood of experiencing our commonality;
and experiencing our commonality supports
further partnering,
and on it goes.

13.
The Love cycle: Part 2

And there is another, critical, feature of the Love cycle.
Connecting with the "other" increases the possibility of our
experiencing our commonality with the "other".
And connecting with the "other" also enables us to experience
the difference of the "other"
as that difference really is –
free of whatever myths, distortions, fantasies, fears, and
projections arise as a consequence of our separateness.
Love supports Love *and* Power.
The possibility of a Love-and-Power cycle emerges,
creating a wholeness to our experience of the "other",
seeing them as the same as us in fundamental ways
and as different from us in fundamental ways,
freeing us to pursue our separate ways
and to join together in ongoing and mutually meaningful ways.
Same and different,
separate and connected,
Relationships of Love and Power.

14.
System blindness, system sight.

The Love and Power cycle *is* a human possibility,
one that enables us to live creatively with difference
without oppression in any of its forms.
Yet, when we are in the grip of system blindness,
the Love and Power cycle is inconceivable.
Not with these people.

So that is our continuing human challenge.
There is the truth about human relationships
and there is our willingness to accept the truth. The truth is:
the patterns we fall into shape our experience;
change the pattern and our experience will change.
Disrupt the Power cycle with Love
and a new experience of the "other" will emerge.
That's the truth.
Do you reject it out of hand?
Do you believe it?
Or are you willing to test it?

15.
The alternative is always at hand:
bigotry, oppression, suppression, exile, and killing.
In the following section there are brief descriptions of
some of the 20th- and 21st-century catastrophes stemming from
Power without Love.
Some are examples of Tolerance solutions devolving into Purity
solutions.
Some are examples of enlightened, high-culture civilizations
falling into barbarism.
All are examples of the triumph of system blindness over
system sight,
the consequences of Power without Love.

Catastrophes:

Power without Love

1.
Sacred missions

Catastrophes are clothed (justified) as sacred missions.

- A perceived sense of long-standing injustice erupts in revenge, resulting in the wholesale slaughter of the perceived oppressors.
- The beliefs, practices, rites and rituals of the "other" are experienced as violating the sacred beliefs, practices, and rituals of the host culture.
- The very existence of the "other" in the territory held sacred by the host culture is experienced as a contaminating influence resulting in the slaughter and expulsion of the "other."
- The host culture develops a new social or political ideology, and the behavior of the "others" is seen as blocking the implementation of that ideology, resulting in the re-education, massacre, or expulsion of the "other".

2.
Demagogues

Demagogues play a major role in inflaming catastrophes,
mobilizing the forces for rejection
by offering a near irresistible appeal:
Purity,
the sacredness of their cause,
the sacredness of the culture they choose to
protect and purify,
the superiority – moral, spiritual, physical –
of those who join them in purifying the culture,
the inferiority – moral, spiritual, physical – of the "other".
The sacred mission is to purify the culture by dominating,
if not eliminating the "other"
and eliminating those who support the "other".

3.
Perpetrator or Victim

Catastrophes are the subject of fierce debate,
depending on whether one's culture has been portrayed
as the perpetrator of the catastrophe
or its victim.

And, sometimes, a culture maintains its image of purity
by denying that the catastrophe has even occurred.
And, sometimes, catastrophes are portrayed not as crimes, but
as realistic outcomes of cultural self-defense and growth.

4.

Whatever protective mythology has been created,
and whatever rationales have been offered,
the Purity solution has been employed
throughout recorded human history,
resulting in the oppression, expulsion, and murder
of hundreds of millions of human beings.

5.

Catastrophes are an imminent possibility
as long as there are cultural differences –
skin color, race, religion, ethnicity, political ideologies –
as long as there are demagogues ready to exploit these
differences,
selling us messages of our superiority and purity
and the inferiority and impurity of the "other",
and so long as we are needy and naïve enough
to take these messages to heart
and fall into relationships in which our experience of the "other"
is grounded in Power without Love.

A Sample of 20th- and 21st-Century Catastrophes

NOTE: The following summary of 20th- and 21st-century catastrophes is incomplete and potentially subject to much dispute. My research was based on internet searches; Wikipedia was a very helpful source. Source estimates of deaths and expulsions vary widely, yet the precision of numbers is not the primary point. What does matter is recognizing our human capacity for reacting viciously and lethally to the "other" in the service of one form of Purity Solution or another.

- **Myanmar (2017 and continuing).** In the service of creating a *Clean and Beautiful Nation,* Muslim Rohingya, although having lived in Myanmar for generations, are treated as separate, non-citizens, illegal immigrants, "Bengalis". As such, they have been driven from their homes and country, forced to live in squatter camps and slums and have been subject to rape, torture, and arson.

- **China (2017 and continuing).** In its purification program, China has not attempted to destroy the Muslim Uighurs of Xinjiang, but it is intent on destroying their culture: detaining over one million in "re-education" centers and not releasing them until they have renounced their beliefs, destroying thousands of their mosques, fining them for having too many children, creating a ban on fasting during Ramadan, promoting (pressuring) intermarriage between Uighur women and Han men, and flooding previously majority Uighur cities with Han settlers.

- **Palestine and Israel (continuing).** Arabs and Jews have been involved in a decades-long struggle for control over the same sliver of Mideast land. From the 1900s and even earlier, there have been regular outbreaks of violence, including massacres. Both sides have engaged in purification campaigns aimed at displacing or eliminating the other: from the Palestinian Nakba in which an estimated 700,000 Palestinian Arabs fled or were expelled from their homes during the 1948 Arab-Israeli war, to the emergence in 1987 of Hamas, whose charter calls for the elimination of Israel and the establishment of an Islamic Palestinian state in its place. In recent years Israeli settlers have expanded into territories considered to be part of a potential Palestinian homeland including its capital. On October 7, 2023, a military wing of Hamas launched a devastating attack on Israel, killing more than 1,400 people, mostly civilians; Israel immediately launched a retaliatory air attack, in the first week killing upwards of 7,500 Palestinians, also largely civilian.

- **Darfur (2003 and continuing).** Government attacks on the villages of Sudan's non-Arab, darker-skinned farmers commonly began with Air Force bombings. These air campaigns were often followed by Janjaweed militia raids in which surviving village men, women, and children were either murdered or forced to flee. It is estimated that this purification campaign has resulted in four million people being displaced and two million dead. Despite changing governments and peace agreements, the murderous rampage against civilian populations continues – raping, pillaging, and leaving corpses on the street to rot.

- **ISIL genocides (1999 and continuing).** A caliphate was created aimed at building a pure Islamic state which would follow the prophecy and example of the prophet in precise detail. The goal of ISIL is to purify the world by destroying all who do not live by these principles; this has included Assyrian Christians in Iraq, Yazidi, Shiites, and the heads of every Muslim country who have elevated man-made law above Sharia. Ongoing worldwide attacks on civilians in many countries are further acts of purification through the deaths of "infidels".

- **Rwanda (1994).** Over a 100-day period, an estimated 500,000 to 1,000,000 Tutsis, approximately 70% of the Tutsi population in Rwanda, were slaughtered through the actions of the Hutu majority government. Soldiers and police officers encouraged ordinary citizens to take part. The extremist Hutu regime appeared to believe that their only hope for maintaining power demanded the complete destruction of ethnic Tutsis.

- **Cambodia (1975-1997).** Somewhere between 1.5 and 3 million Cambodians were killed in a vision-driven attempt to create a new society – an ideal socialist agrarian republic based on Marxist-Leninist and Maoist principles. The effort required a total societal transformation including the creation of a "new man". Mass killings were organized of those opposed to or seen as unfit for this new world – ethnic minorities, intellectuals and professionals, civil servants, and recalcitrant city dwellers.

- **The Partition of India (1947).** Hindus, Muslims, and Sikhs who had co-existed for a millennium attacked each other in efforts to purify their newly separated states. The members of two states were bent on destroying one another through horrific acts of violence. Gangs of killers were reported to have set whole villages aflame, hacking to death men and children and the aged while carrying off young women to be raped.

- **Croatia (1941).** In the service of establishing a "Greater Croatia", an estimated 500,000 Serbs were murdered, 250,000 expelled, and 200,000 forcibly converted to Catholicism. (Estimates vary widely.) Most atrocities occurred in several concentration camps throughout Croatia. Serbs, identified with blue badges, were often murdered immediately upon arrival.

- **Armenia (during World War I).** The Ottoman government, followed by its successor Turkish government, systematically exterminated 1.5 million Christian Armenians. The campaign began in 1915 with the roundup, arrest, and deportation of Armenian intellectuals and community leaders, the majority of whom were eventually murdered. The Armenian holocaust is an example of a decades long Tolerance solution that devolved into Catastrophe.

- **Germany (1942-1945).** At the height of its power, Germany controlled territory in countries with extensive pre-war Jewish populations: Germany and Austria (240,000 Jews), Poland (3,300,000), the Baltic nations (253,000), Slovakia (90,000), Greece (70,000), the Netherlands (140,000), Hungary (650,000), Soviet States (1,875,000), Belgium (65,000), Yugoslavia (43,000), Romania (600,000), Norway (2,170), France (350,000), Bulgaria (64,000), Italy (40,000), Luxembourg (5,000), Russian SFSR (975,000), Denmark (8,000). Of the 8,861,800 Jews living in these countries, 5,933,900 (67%) were murdered, often with the willful collaboration of these countries' citizens.

I am aware of so many catastrophes I have not included, some of which I will mention in a phrase or two simply to emphasize the breadth and depth of catastrophe as a human possibility.

- **The Nazi Eugenics,** between 1939 and 1941, 80,000 to 100,000 mentally ill adults in institutions, 5,000 children in institutions, and 1,000 Jews in institutions were killed.

- **The Polish genocide.** In preparation for the occupation of Poland, an anti-intelligentsia action resulted in the murder of 100,000 Polish citizens. The goal was to complete the Germanization of western regions of Poland before being settled by *pure* Aryans.

- **Genocide of the Slavic population in the Soviet Union.** As central to their plan (lebensraum) of expansion eastward and creating a New Order in Europe, the Nazis set about purifying their new territory by enslaving, expelling, and destroying the Slavic peoples of Europe whom they considered racially inferior and non-Aryan. The death toll in areas occupied by Germany was estimated at 13.7 million.

- **The Expulsion of Muslims.** In the 1860s, the Russian Tsar ordered the expulsion of most of the Muslim population of the North Caucasus in order to have access to the Black Sea coast. A whole population was eliminated in order to satisfy the economic interests of a powerful country.

- **Algeria.** 1830-1875. The French conquered Algeria and attempted to purify it (making it French) by killing an estimated 825,000 indigenous Algerians.

- **Democratic Republic of Congo.** During the Civil War, there was a program called *Effacer le tableau* (wipe the slate clean) aimed at purifying the country by destroying the pygmy population.

- **North America.** From the 1490s into the 1900s, native Americans were uprooted from their lands, subject to forced relocations, massacres, torture, and sexual abuse. Practice of their religion was outlawed, children were taken from their families in an effort to "educate" them away their culture.

- **Ireland.** 1650s. The native population of Ireland was forcibly displaced as part of the mission to transfer the land from Irish to English hands.

- **Sri Lanka.** 1983-2000. Genocide of the minority Hindu Tamils at the hands of the primarily Buddhist government.

- **East Timor.** 1975 onward. During the occupation of East Timor by Indonesia, the government tried to purify the country by killing, causing death from hunger and illness, and using starvation as a weapon to exterminate the East Timorese. Estimates of death ranged from 60,000 to 200,000.

- **Indonesia.** 1965-1966. The Indonesian government, with the support of Great Britain, Australia, and the United States, aided and abetted mass killings including beheading, evisceration, dismemberment, and castration of hundreds of thousands of leftists and those tied to the Communist Party.

- **North Korea.** Continuing. In an effort to purify the state, the Christian population of North Korea has been systematically massacred and persecuted; by 2012, 50,000-70,000 Christians were imprisoned in North Korea's concentration camps.

- **Bangladesh Liberation War.** During the 1971 war for independence, members of the Pakistani military supported by Islamist militias raped 200,000-400,000 Bangladeshi women and girls in a systematic campaign of genocidal rape.

- **Polish Ukrainian genocide.** 1943-1945. The Ukrainian Insurgent Army killed 40,000-60,000 Polish civilians in Volhynia and 25,000-40,000 in Eastern Galicia for the purpose of removing non-Ukrainians from a future purified Ukrainian state.

- The **Srebrenica massacre.** 1995. The massacre of more than 8,000 Muslim Bosniaks, mainly men and boys, perpetrated by units of the Bosnian Serb army and assisted by the Scorpions, a paramilitary unit from Serbia,

- **The Holdomor.** From 1930 to 1937 an estimated 7-10 million Russian peasants died of starvation resulting from the elimination of kulaks – rich land-owning peasant farmers – who were shot or deported and whose lands were collectivized. People standing in the way of a sacred socialist mission.

Enough.

So, there it is.
Purity is one solution to encountering the "other",
and Tolerance another.
Both are grounded in varying degrees of Power over Love.
Both exact their terrible costs on the oppressed
while diminishing the humanity of the oppressors.

And there is a third possibility,
one that requires a fundamental transformation in
how we *see* and *experience* one another,
a transformation based on the understanding that:
the interaction patterns we fall into
shape how we see and experience one another.
What seems to be a real and solid picture of the "other"
is merely the consequence of the pattern we have fallen into.
Change the pattern of interaction
and our experiences of one another will change.

The possibility *of Power **and** Love will emerge.*

Afterword

Encounters with the Other is a long-delayed response to a child's plea upon learning of the horrors of the Holocaust: *How can people do this to one another?* It is a plea that could be heard both as anger (How can people be so cruel, so ignorant?) and as curiosity (How does this hate develop? How does it begin?) *Encounters with the Other* is my answer to that plea. It contains deep and simple truths about ourselves – our vulnerabilities and our creative possibilities.

The big promise of *Encounters with the Other* is that it has the potential to end the long chain of oppressions of "Others". How does that happen? It happens when every child in the world – along with learning their letters and numbers and songs and games – learns about the oppression of "Others"; the children learn it through stories, songs, and dramas. They learn it in the histories of other times and places and in the history of their own culture. They learn how it begins and how it can end. The learning will be powerful; children may weep in pain and sorrow…and determination. Inquiry and anger. *Never again!*

That's how it *can* end.

But will it?

The children may never see *Encounters with the Other* nor learn any of its lessons, for there are those whose existence rests on the continued oppression of the "Other", any "Other". The Narcissist who, in his love of self, would sacrifice all others to protect his image as Life's perpetual Winner, the Demagogue who wields the key that unlocks the crowd's fury; the Masters of Social Media whose wealth rests on inciting us to hate and fear one another.

But ultimately, the future of the oppression of the "Other" rests on us – on our gullibility, vulnerability, ignorance, stupidity, mindlessness – we who worship in ecstasy at the altar of the Narcissist (seen as God or sent by God); we who rally round the Demagogue, happily wearing his uniform as he urges us on to hate some "Other"; and we who gather round our dumbphones, drinking in their mind-numbing poisons as if manna from heaven.

So, what is the antidote?

Awareness. WAKE UP! The Oppression of the "Other" happens only when we are sleepwalking, and it will end only when we waken to the truth. The Narcissist does not love *us*; he loves only himself. The Demagogue is driven not by *our* needs but by his needs for power. And the Masters of Social Media measure the meaning of life not by truth but by the number of likes and clicks.

Awareness is the antidote. To be able to recognize these tricks and ploys and manipulations as they offer up to us some "Other" to fear, hate, avoid, and oppress. And awareness gives us the magnificent and powerful gift of choice: to go down the path of hate, or to reply: *Sorry, I don't go there, I have other business, I am here to teach the children.*

Barry Oshry, Centerville, Massachusetts, U.S.A.
September 2023

About the Author

Barry Oshry is a pioneer in the field of human systems thinking. His life's work has been to empower individuals and organizations by transforming system-blindness into system-sight. The educational programs he has developed include The Power Lab, the Organization Workshop on Creating Partnership, and the When Cultures Meet Workshop.

In 1975 he and his wife and partner, Karen Ellis Oshry, founded Power+Systems, Inc. whose worldwide network of trainers continues the work of empowering individuals and organizations by transforming system-blindness into system-sight. They retired from Power+Systems in 2018.

In 2013 he launched The Worldwide Week of Partnership, during which Power+Systems trainers across the globe conduct pro bono partnership events for educational, charitable, advocacy, and service organizations in their local communities. In 2015 he received a Lifetime Achievement Award from the International Organization Development Network.

Barry is the author of *The Systems Letter, Seeing Systems, Leading Systems, In the Middle, The Possibilities of Organization,* and *Context, Context, Context.* He is also a playwright whose stage productions include "What a Way to Make a Living", "Hierarchy", "Power Play", and "Peace".

Barry's latest book is *Context, Context, Context.* See:
www.triarchypress.net/context or
http://store.powerandsystems.com

oshrybarry@gmail.com
www.powerandsystems.com
www.worldwideweekofpartnership.org

About the Publisher

Triarchy Press is a small independent publisher of books that bring a wider, systemic or contextual approach to many different areas of life, including:

Government, Education, Health and other public services
Ecology, Sustainability and Regenerative Cultures
Leading and Managing Organizations
Psychotherapy and Arts and other Expressive Therapies
The Money System
Walking, Psychogeography and Mythogeography
Movement and Somatics
Innovation
The Future and Future Studies

For books by Barry Oshry, John Seddon, Nora Bateson, Daniel Wahl, Miranda Tufnell, Russ Ackoff, Phil Smith, Linda Hartley, Bill Tate, Sandra Reeve, Graham Leicester, Alyson Hallett and other remarkable writers, please visit:

www.triarchypress.net

Praise for *Encounters*

"This writing is a gift! *Encounters with the Other* must be placed in every teacher's and student's hands beginning as early as 6th or 7th grade, woven into their history and social studies programs to help future generations recognize the signs that keep repeating themselves around the world and in our own communities."
Lily Bowen, VP Leadership & OD at Travelers Insurance, USA

"Thank you so much for this. I read it all and it moved me to tears. There is so much that needs to be done and sometimes the task seems hopeless, but we need to keep striving and, in the process, making small changes that will hopefully grow into a powerful wave of 'humanity.'"
Salman Ahmad, Lecturer at Copenhagen Business School, Denmark

"At the end of this little book, Barry Oshry says there's a middle way of building community –- not pure power or love, but mutual self-awareness. That's been the core theme of his work ever since *Seeing Systems*: watching people shift roles from Top to Bottom to Middle to Customer. They see their own behavior shift accordingly, and that's the first step. Barry has been a prophet of systems awareness for all his career."
Art Kleiner, Author of *The Age of Heretics* and *The Wise Advocate*

"Wow, what an inspiring and much needed project."
Kara Penfield, Center for Creative Leadership, USA

"Clear, moving, sad and hopeful all in one!"
Simon Allen, Principal Lumina Consulting, UK

"A moving thoughtful perspective on how we create the 'other,' by blindly falling into patterns that negate our and their full humanity. We need this wise reminder of who we are and what we individually and collectively can become...and that it is a choice."
Don Jones, Founder and President, Experience It, Inc., Canada

"[A] beautiful piece of work. So crystal clear, so enlightening, and infused with so much humanity. A call to arms for all of us."
Paul Mitchell, Founder at The Human Enterprise, Australia

"A wholeness resulting from a cycle of Love and Power, which allows us to see both the similarities and differences with others as they really are, is a profound insight. Balancing the forces of Power and Love is the most important work we can do as individuals and as a society."
George B. Forsythe, Ph.D., Brigadier General, U.S. Army (retd.)

"Oshry's beautifully crafted thesis sheds light on a path forward. It is a hard path, a path many will not choose to see, but for those of us seeking community, love, and learning, the path he illuminates is the journey of our lifetimes."
Helene T. Roos, Psy.D, Founder/President HAD Consulting

"Written in the style of an epic poem, this is a lament for what ails the modern world and, in particular, the way we treat each other as means and not ends; and it is a moving elegy for a world yet to be created, where love matches power."
Jules Goddard, Fellow, London Business School

"A brilliant and creative piece of writing. I like the format because the key points are easily 'digested' and organized in a coherent and logical flow."
David Altman, COO, Center for Creative Leadership, USA

"Oshry describes so simply, so clearly, core dynamics of being in relation with others – the dynamics that are just as relevant in one-on-one relationships as between two cultures. The power in revealing these patterns is that once you see them, they are hard to forget."

Naryan Wong, Network Weaver, Toronto, Canada

"This may be some of Barry Oshry's clearest and most insightful writing. It has a precision and subtlety of how 'encounters with the other' often go that merits careful study and digestion."

John Watters, Managing Director at Living Leadership, UK

"A masterpiece. A visceral journey to a new place of understanding. Its time is now."

Deb Travers-Wolf, Founder/ CEO I LEAD Consulting, Sydney, Australia

"This is so elegantly written. Love it.....Congratulations on so many levels.....Truly inspiring clarity and vision."

Kevin Purcell, USA

"A wonderful way to see the patterns that drive us individually and as communities. It is also uncomfortable reading, seeing ourselves naked, shorn of our coverings of justification and self-righteousness. The list of 'catastrophes' at the end is by no means exhaustive and should make us sick to our stomachs. If anything will shock us into using the energy of Love not Power this must be it."

Nick Smith, UK

"Extraordinarily important"

Bob Stilger, Founder at New Stories, USA

"I really appreciate the parable/poetry/essay/social science Encounters. Nicely done."

Bill Kahn, Professor at Boston University, USA

"Barry Oshry, despite his esteem in certain circles, is perhaps the most under-appreciated thinker of our times with regard to human organisation and society. I have often wondered why this is the case, and my conclusion is that this is because he has gone deeper and found a purer essence than most. So, I have only one exhortation for those lucky enough to read this: see this prose poem not as perspective or opinion, but as a scientific project; an attempt to divine a deep human truth, through observation and theory. See the dynamics he identifies as fundamental building blocks, as a true paradigm of human behaviour. To do so is illuminating and empowering."

Benjamin P. Taylor, Managing Partner, RedQuadrant, U.K

"Barry Oshry is one of those rare and intriguing characters: an actual original thinker. For years he has done groundbreaking research on what makes us tick. The answer, it turns out, is that our personalities are shaped far more than we might like by the systems we live in. The challenge, then, is to understand and master these conditions to live a healthy and productive life."

Adi Ignatius, Editor in Chief, *Harvard Business Review*

"Thank you so much for sharing this beautiful and powerful work! I just read it and have to confess that it ignited a fire within me…"

Alexandre Costa, Director at Integraal, Brazil

"The poetic language takes the reader to a deeper level of understanding of power AND love…Oshry displays an impressive ability to simplify complex and abstract theories…Humbling and inspiring. Many thanks for your dedication to solving our broken systems."

Nancy Haller, Ph.D., Organizational Psychologist, San Diego, California

"A delightful way of conveying emotionally charged topics that enables the reader to let down one's guard."

Mitchell Karp, USA

"In ... *Encounters with the Other*, Barry Oshry offers us a framework to think about how we connect with "the other". It's a timely offering, given how much conflict and suffering there is, and has been, in the world over the 20th and 21st centuries. His thought-piece is a moving "cri de coeur", calling on all of us to examine our beliefs about "the other" and how we dehumanize them – to get beyond simple tolerance and to open our hearts to them. Oshry invites us to look inward and to examine our projections based on fear and desire, to put us on the path to getting to know "the other". It is not just that our solutions often diminish the oppressed, he argues, but that they also "diminish the oppressors (us), corrupting and de-humanizing them (us), as they hang their self-worth on the fragile thread of the diminished worth of the 'other'". This appeal to our higher selves could not be more urgent".

Abby Yanow, President, Boston Facilitators Roundtable

Milton Keynes UK
Ingram Content Group UK Ltd.
UKHW021824181223
434609UK00019B/1419